SHANIA TWAIN

CONTENTS

ISBN 0-634-00473-5

HAL•LEONARD® CORPORATION

7777 W. BLUEMOUND RD. P.O. BOX 13819 MILWAUKEE, WI 53213

For all works contained herein:
Unauthorized copying, arranging, adapting, recording or public performance is an infringement of copyright.
Infringers are liable under the law.

Visit Hal Leonard Online at
www.halleonard.com

ANY MAN OF MINE

Words and Music by SHANIA TWAIN
and R.J. LANGE

Copyright © 1995 Songs Of PolyGram International, Inc., Loon Echo, Inc. and Out Of Pocket Productions Ltd.
All Rights on behalf of Out Of Pocket Productions Ltd. Controlled by Zomba Enterprises Inc. for the U.S. and Canada
International Copyright Secured   All Rights Reserved

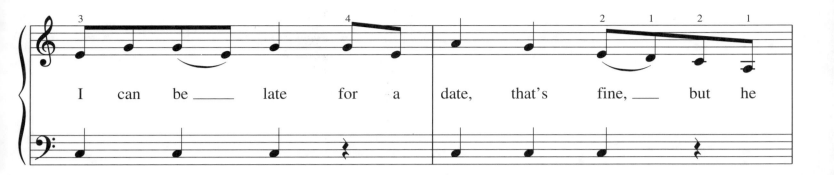

I can be ___ late for a date, that's fine, ___ but he

C5

bet - ter be ___ on time. ___ And | an - y man of mine-'ll say it
 | an - y man of mine bet - ter

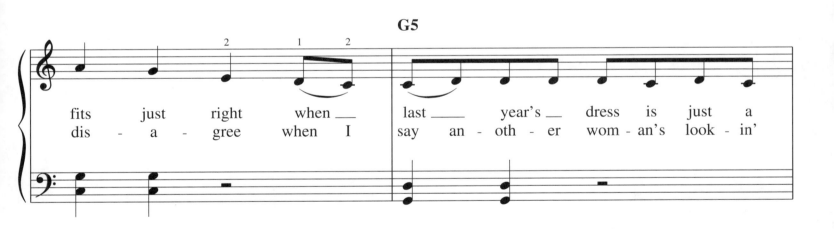

G5

fits just right when ___ last ___ year's ___ dress is just a
dis - a - gree when I say an - oth - er wom - an's look - in'

C5

lit - tle too ___ tight. And an - y - thing I do or say bet - ter
bet - ter than ___ me. And when I cook him din - ner and I

4

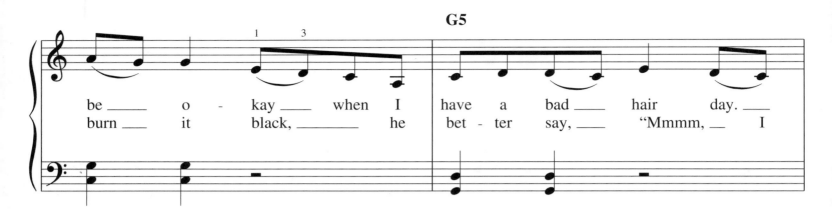

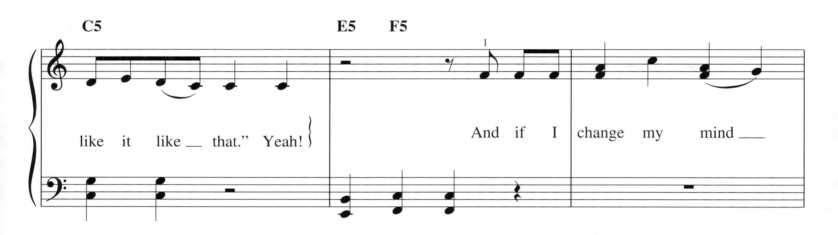

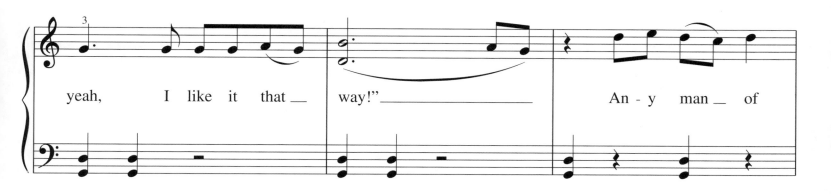

yeah,   I   like   it   that __   way!" _____   An - y   man __   of

F   **C**

mine   bet - ter   walk   the   line. _____

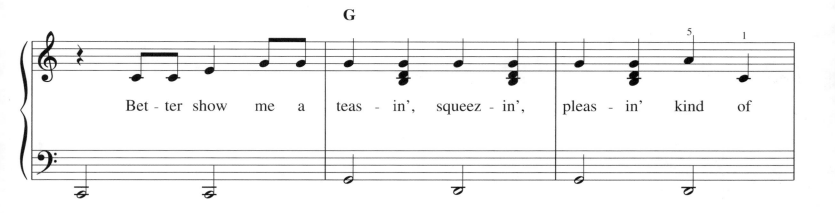

G

Bet - ter   show   me   a   teas - in',   squeez - in',   pleas - in'   kind   of

C   **F**

time.   I   need   a   man   who   knows

D.S. al Coda

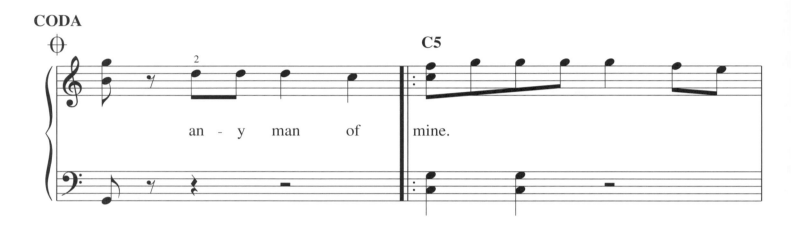

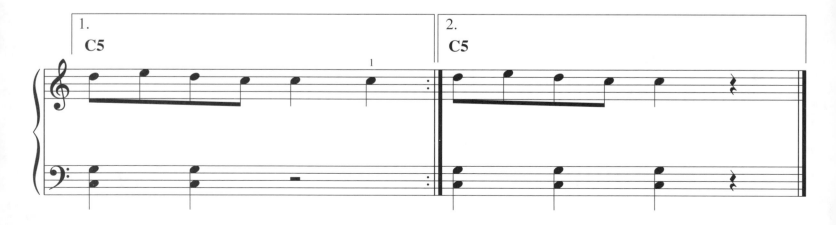

HOME AIN'T WHERE HIS HEART IS ANYMORE

Words and Music by SHANIA TWAIN
and R.J. LANGE

Slowly

He knew__ how to reach me deep in-

side, _____ and he found a part of me I could not

hide. _____ And we'd walk and talk and touch ten-der-

Copyright © 1995 Songs Of PolyGram International, Inc., Loon Echo, Inc. and Out Of Pocket Productions Ltd.
All Rights on behalf of Out Of Pocket Productions Ltd. Controlled by Zomba Enterprises Inc. for the U.S. and Canada
International Copyright Secured   All Rights Reserved

DON'T BE STUPID
(You Know I Love You)

Words and Music by SHANIA TWAIN
and R.J. LANGE

Copyright © 1997 Songs Of PolyGram International, Inc., Loon Echo, Inc. and Out Of Pocket Productions Ltd.
All Rights on behalf of Out Of Pocket Productions Ltd. Controlled by Zomba Enterprises Inc. for the U.S. and Canada
International Copyright Secured   All Rights Reserved

read my mail. _ I don't ap - pre - ci - ate it. When I

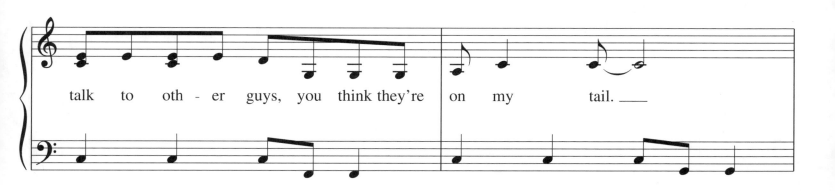

talk to oth - er guys, you think they're on my tail. ___

I

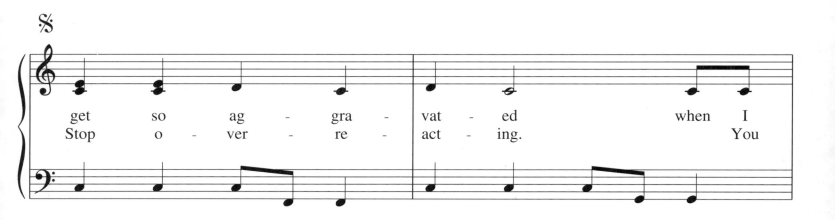

get so ag - gra - vat - ed when I
Stop o - ver - re - act - ing. You

get off the phone __ and get the | third de - gree. __ I'm real - ly
e - ven get sus - pi - cious when I | paint my nails. __ It's

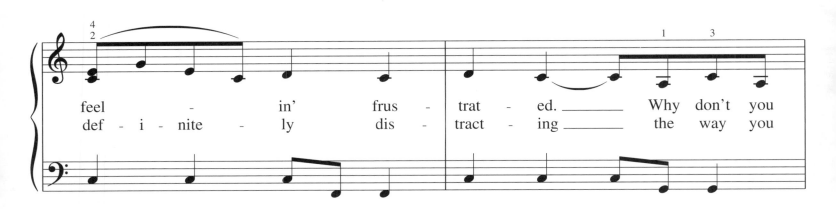

feel - in' frus - trat - ed. _____ Why don't you
def - i - nite - ly dis - tract - ing _____ the way you

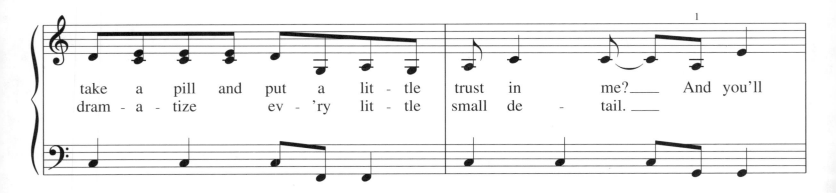

take a pill and put a lit - tle | trust in me? ___ And you'll
dram - a - tize ev - 'ry lit - tle | small de - tail. ___

F   C

see. | Don't freak out un - til you know the
| Don't freak out un - til you know the

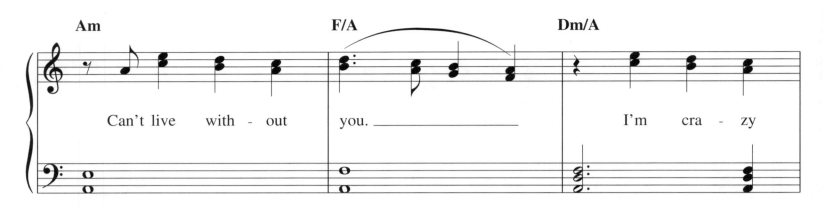

Am — Can't live with - out / F/A — you. _____ / Dm/A — I'm cra - zy

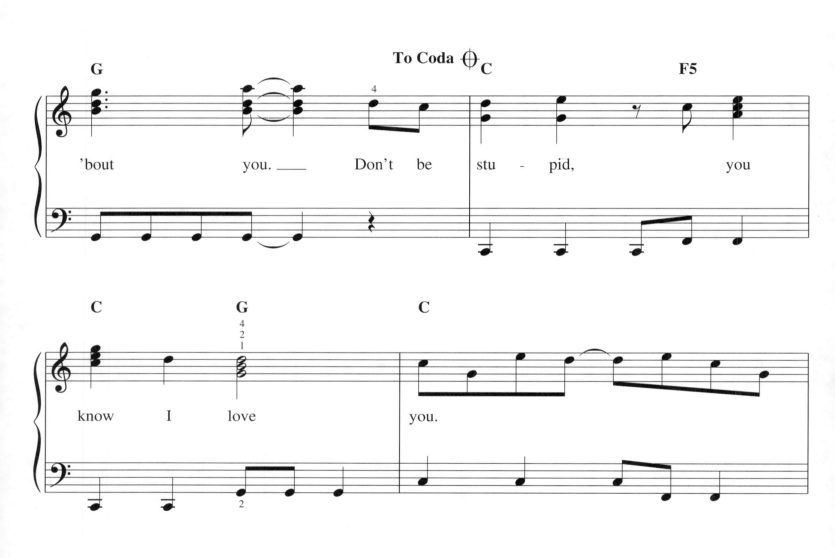

G — 'bout you. ____ Don't be stu - pid, / To Coda C — you / F5

C — know I love / G / C — you.

D.S. al Coda

hair went flat, man, I hate that. Hate that.

Just ___

F7

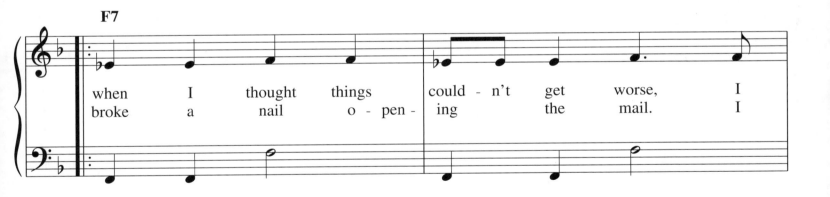

when I thought things could-n't get worse, I
broke a nail o-pen-ing the mail. I

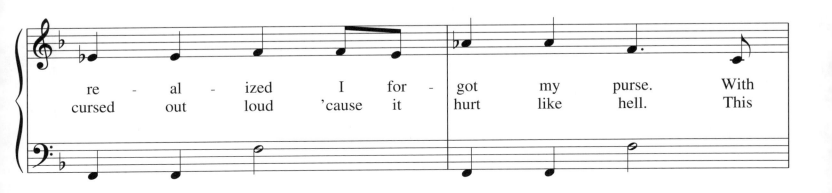

re - al - ized I for - got my purse. With
cursed out loud 'cause it hurt like hell. This

all   this   stress,   I _____   must   con - fess   this
job's   a   pain,   it's   so   mun - dane.   It

B♭

could   be   worse   than __   P   M   S. ____   This   job   ain't
sure   don't   stim - u -   late   my   brain. _

worth   the   pay. _____   Can't   wait   till   the   end   of   the   day. _____

C

Hey,   hon - ey,   I'm   on   my __ way.   Hey!   Hey!

Hey!   Hey!   Hey!   Hey!   Hey! ___   Hon - ey,   I'm   home   and   I

had   a   hard   day.   Pour   me   a   cold   one   and,   oh,   by   the   way,

rub   my   feet,   gim - me   some-thing   to   eat. ___   Fix   me   up   my

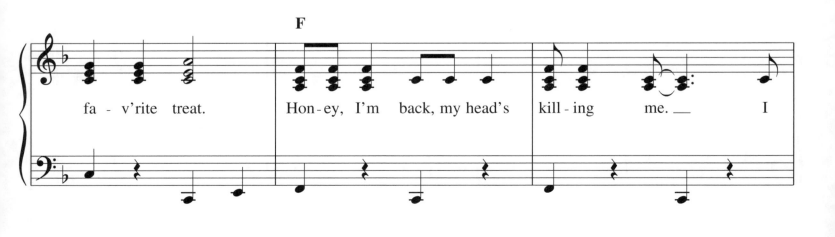

fa - v'rite   treat.   Hon - ey,   I'm   back,   my   head's   kill - ing   me. ___   I

need to re - lax ___ and watch T V. Get off the __ phone, give the

To Coda ⊕

dog a bone. Hey! Hey! Hey! Hey, hon - ey, I'm ___

1.

F7

home.

N.C.

2.

F

I home.

34

YOU WIN MY LOVE

Words and Music by
R.J. LANGE

Moderately fast Rock

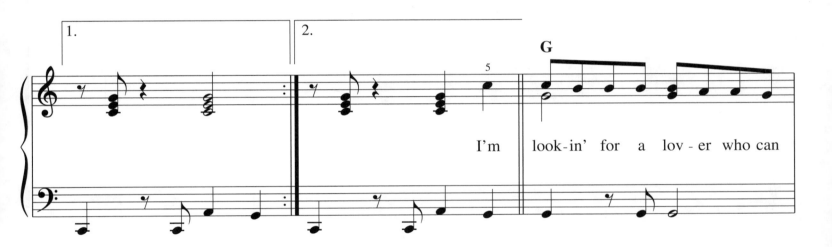

I'm look-in' for a lov-er who can

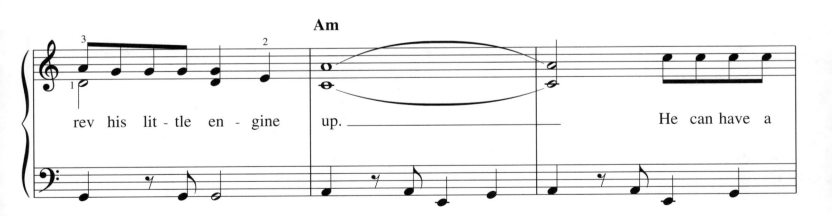

rev his lit-tle en-gine up. _____ He can have a

Copyright © 1995 Out Of Pocket Productions Ltd.
All Rights on behalf of Out Of Pocket Productions Ltd. Controlled by Zomba Enterprises Inc. for the U.S. and Canada
International Copyright Secured   All Rights Reserved

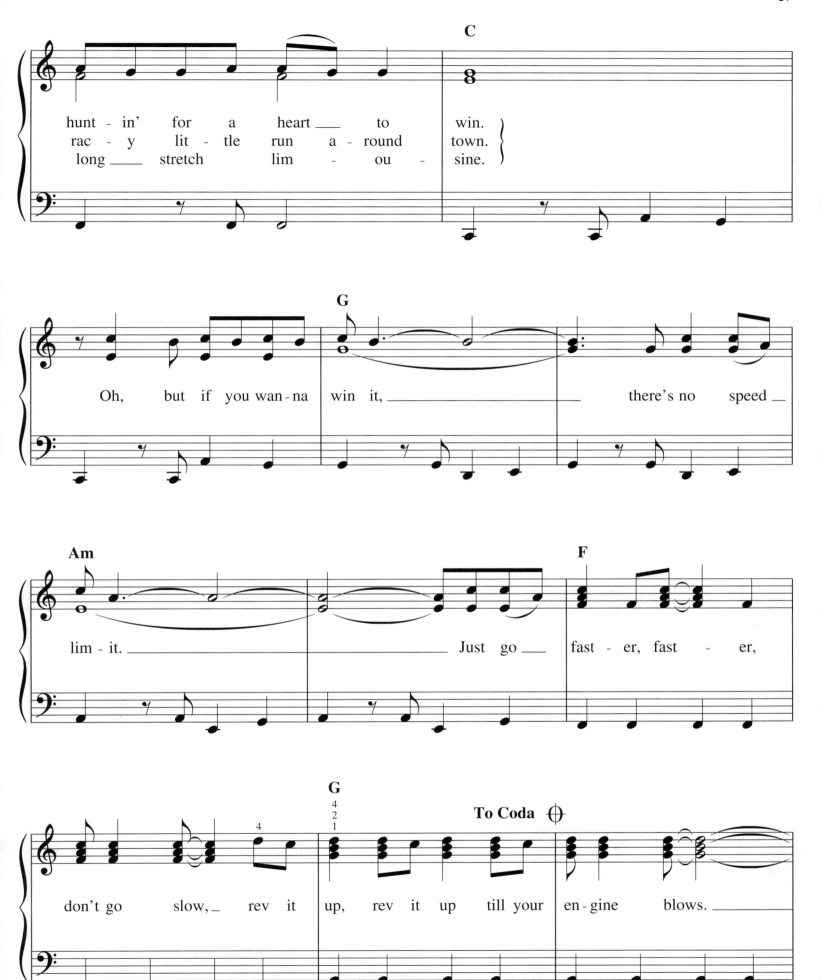

39

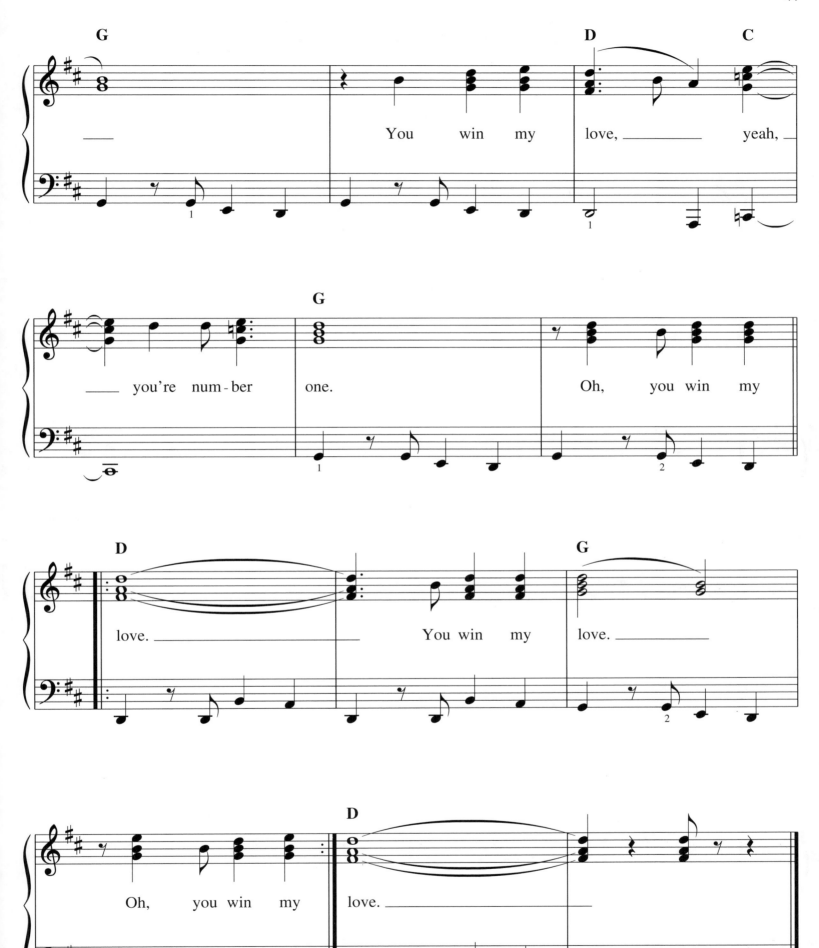

(If You're Not In It for Love)
I'M OUTTA HERE!

Words and Music by SHANIA TWAIN
and R.J. LANGE

Moderately fast Rock

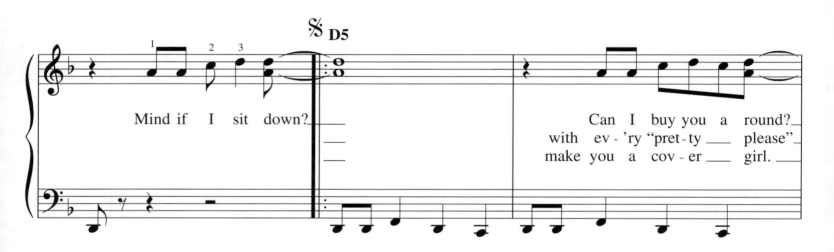

Mind if I sit down?

Can I buy you a round?
with ev - 'ry "pret-ty ___ please"
make you a cov-er ___ girl.

Have - n't seen your face ___
there's a pair of ly- ly-
Yeah, you could be a beau-

Copyright © 1995 Songs Of PolyGram International, Inc., Loon Echo, Inc. and Out Of Pocket Productions Ltd.
All Rights on behalf of Out Of Pocket Productions Ltd. Controlled by Zomba Enterprises Inc. for the U.S. and Canada
International Copyright Secured   All Rights Reserved

44

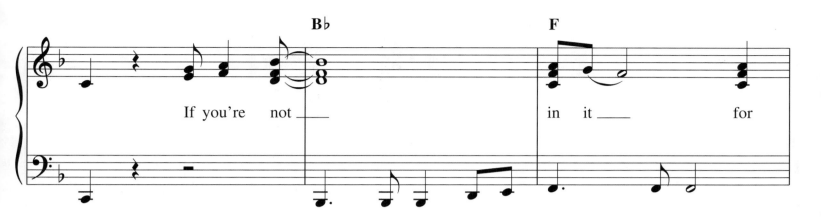

If you're not ____ in it ____ for

love, _____ if you're not ____

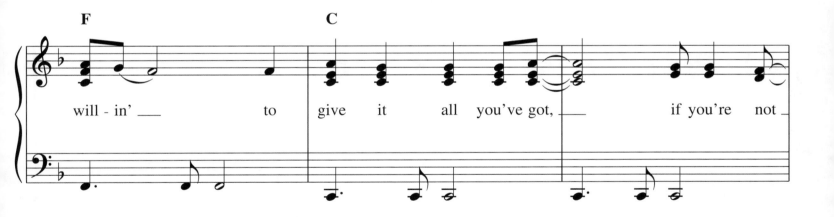

will - in' ____ to give it all you've got, ____ if you're not

____ in it for life, if you're not ____ in it for

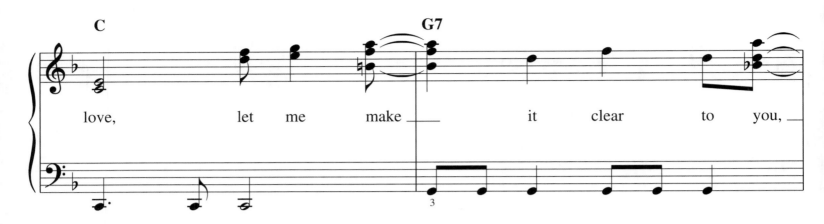

love,   let me make   it clear   to you,

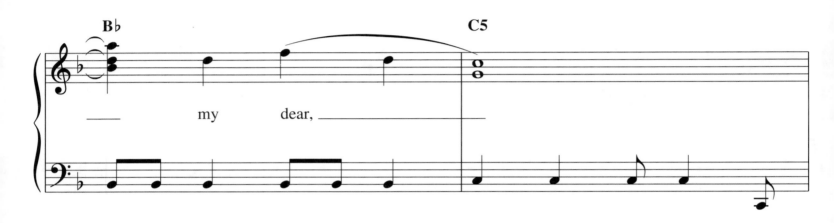

my   dear,

if you're not   in it for love,   I'm out - ta   here.

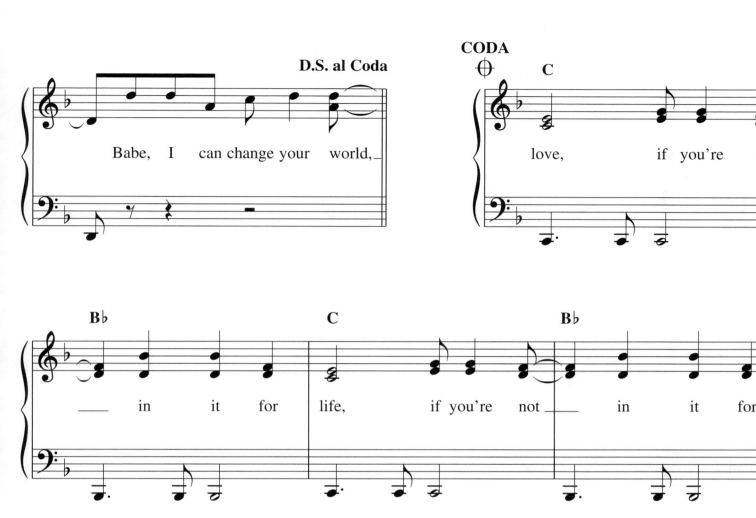

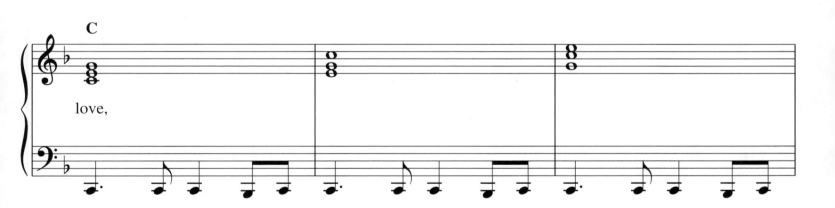

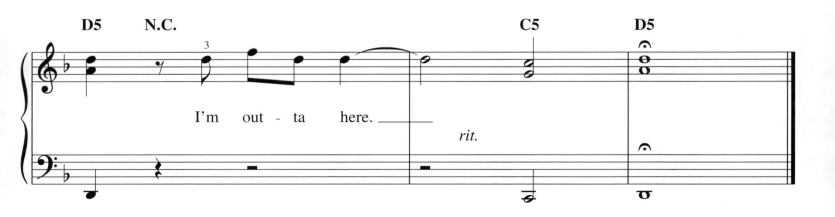

LOVE GETS ME EVERY TIME

Words and Music by SHANIA TWAIN
and R.J. LANGE

Life was go-in' great, love was gon-na have to wait, was in no
I was quite con-tent just a - pay-in' my own rent. It was

(D.S.) *Instrumental solo*

hur - ry, _____ had no wor - ries. _____ Stay - in'
my place, _____ I need - ed my space. _____ I was

Copyright © 1997 Songs Of PolyGram International, Inc., Loon Echo, Inc. and Out Of Pocket Productions Ltd.
All Rights on behalf of Out Of Pocket Productions Ltd. Controlled by Zomba Enterprises Inc. for the U.S. and Canada
International Copyright Secured   All Rights Reserved

sin - gle was the plan, did - n't need a stead - y man; I had it
free to shop a - round, in no rush to set - tle down; I had it

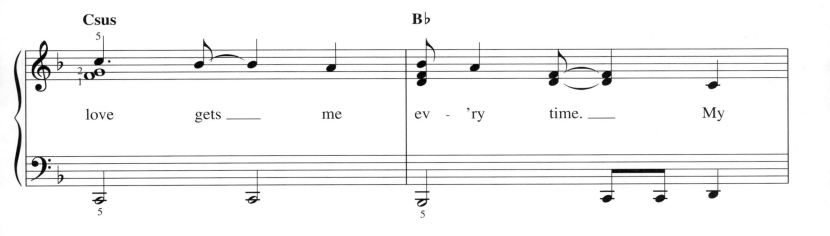

cov - ered _____ 'til I dis - cov - ered _____ }
cov - ered _____ 'til I dis - cov - ered _____ } that
Solo ends

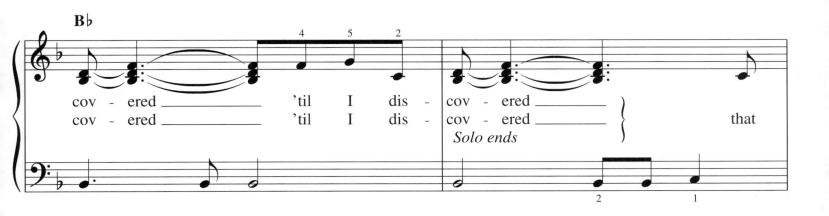

love gets ___ me ev - 'ry time. ___ My

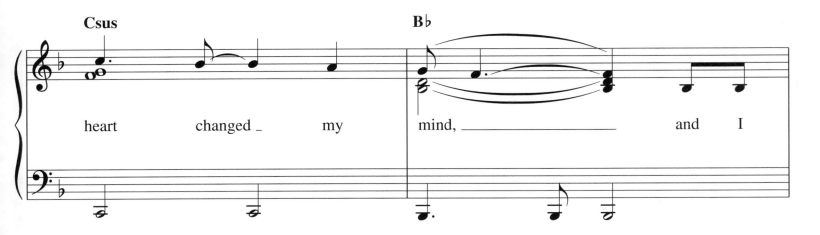

heart changed _ my mind, _____ and I

50

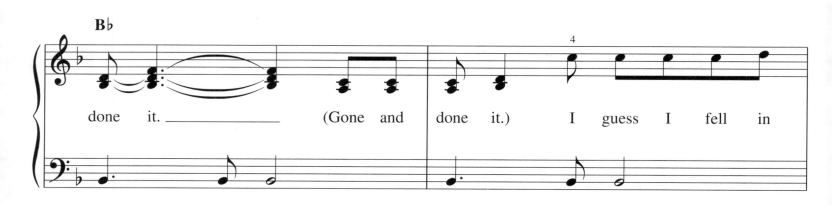

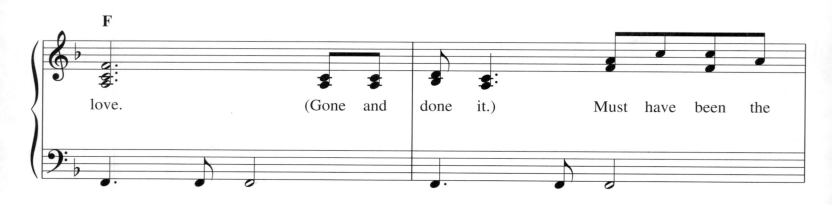

51

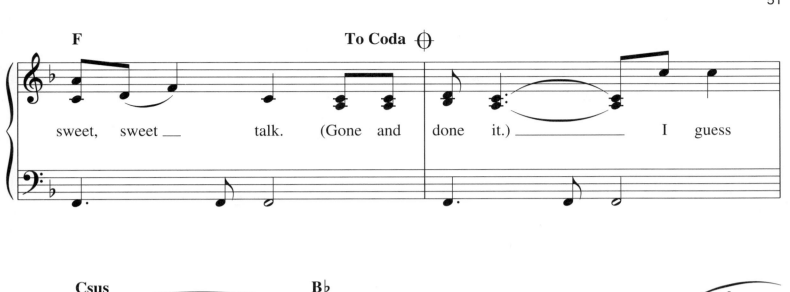

sweet, sweet ___ talk. (Gone and done it.) ___ I guess

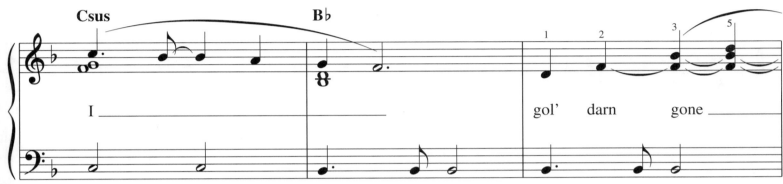

I ___ gol' darn gone ___

___ and done it.

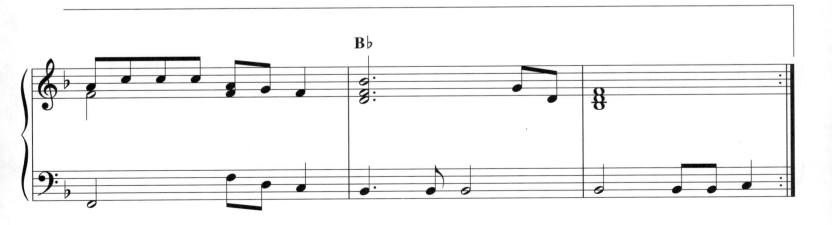

52

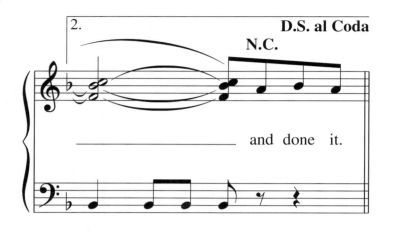

D.S. al Coda

N.C.

_____ and done it.

CODA

done it.) It's in the way he

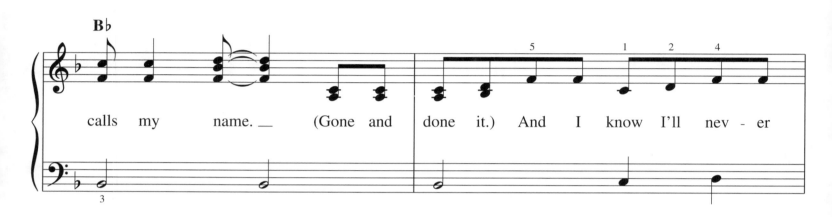

B♭

calls my name. __ (Gone and done it.) And I know I'll nev - er

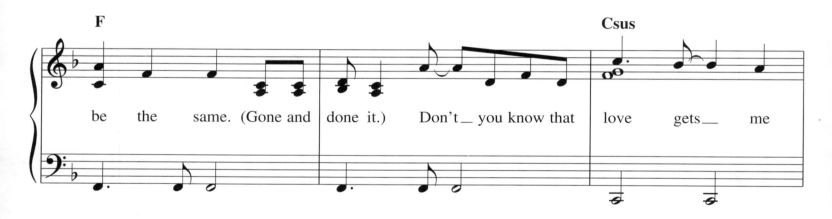

F

Csus

be the same. (Gone and done it.) Don't __ you know that love gets __ me

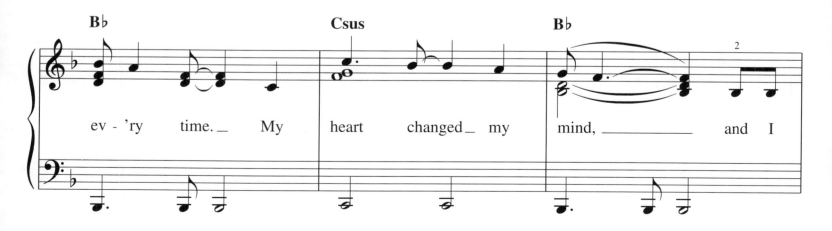

B♭

Csus

B♭

ev - 'ry time. __ My heart changed __ my mind, _____ and I

gol' darn gone _____ and done it.

Thought I had it

cov - ered. _____ Life was go - in' great.

Well, I gol' darn gone and done it. _____

NO ONE NEEDS TO KNOW

Words and Music by SHANIA TWAIN
and R.J. LANGE

Lively Shuffle

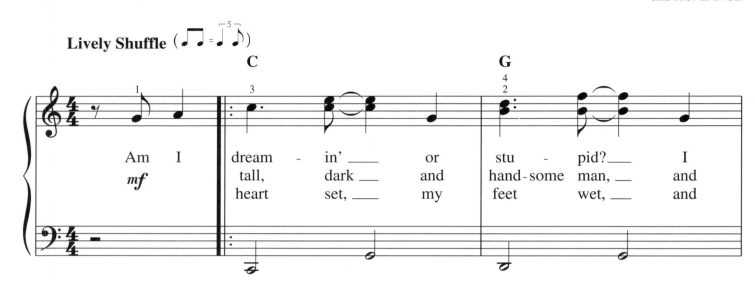

Am I | dream - in' ___ or | stu - pid? ___ I

think I've been hit by | Cu - pid, ___ but | no one needs to
I've been bus - y mak - in' | big plans, ___ but | no one needs to
he don't ___ e - ven | know yet, ___ but | no one needs to

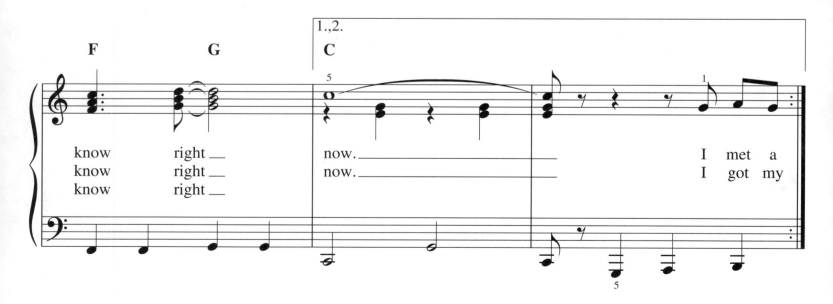

know right ___ | now. ___ | I met a
know right ___ | now. ___ | I got my
know right ___ |

Copyright © 1995 Songs Of PolyGram International, Inc., Loon Echo, Inc. and Out Of Pocket Productions Ltd.
All Rights on behalf of Out Of Pocket Productions Ltd. Controlled by Zomba Enterprises Inc. for the U.S. and Canada
International Copyright Secured   All Rights Reserved

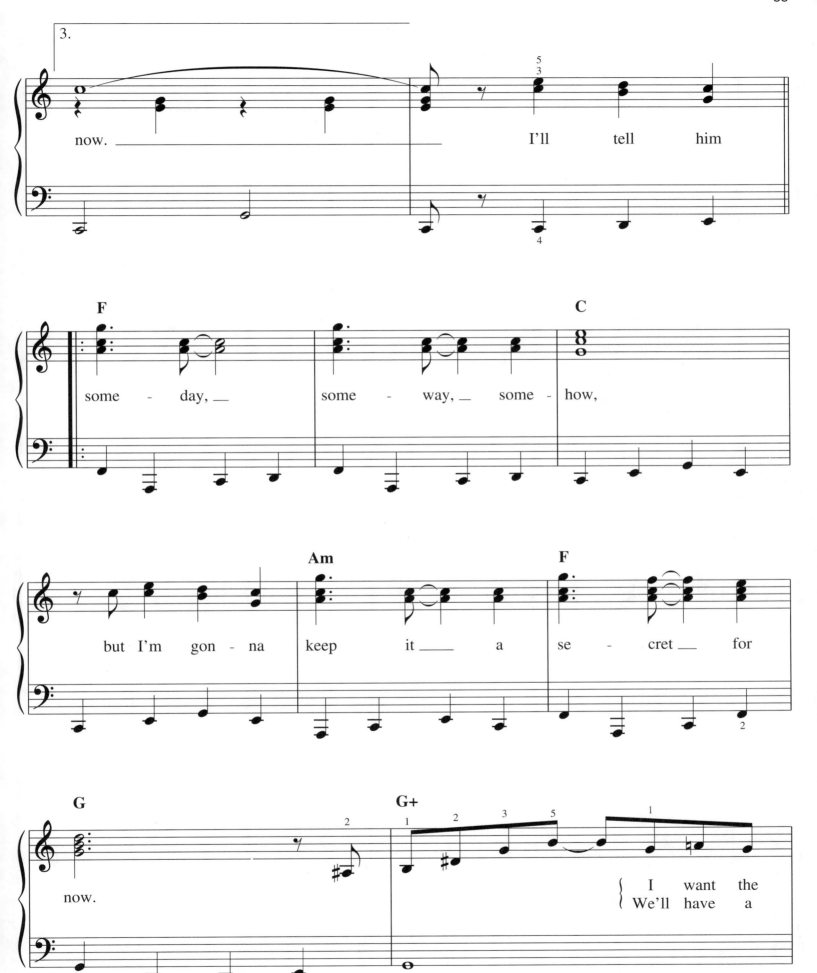

3.

now. _____ I'll tell him

F   C

some - day, ___ some - way, ___ some - how,

Am   F

but I'm gon - na keep it ___ a se - cret ___ for

G   G+

now.   { I want the
                            { We'll have a

56

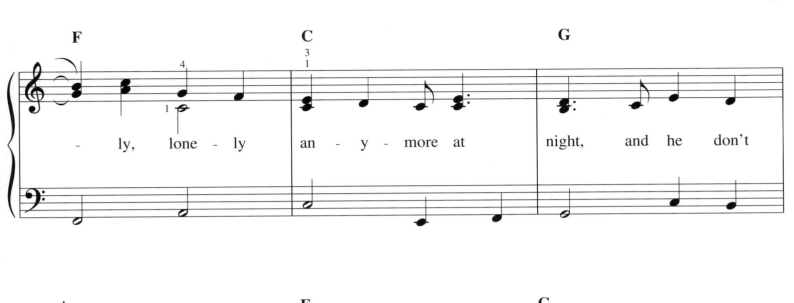

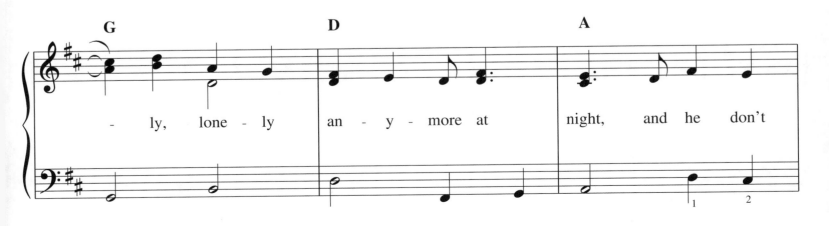

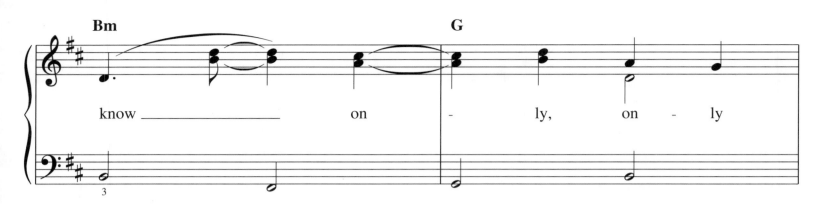

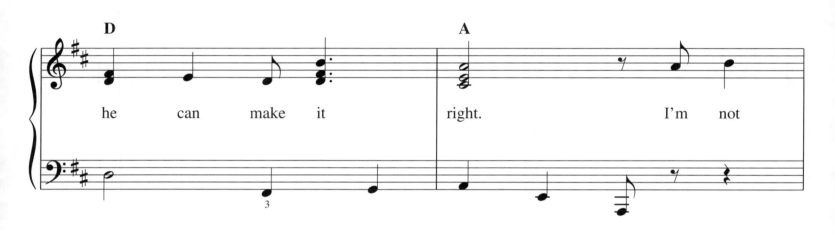

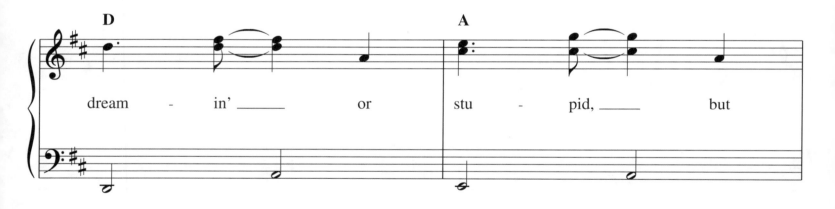

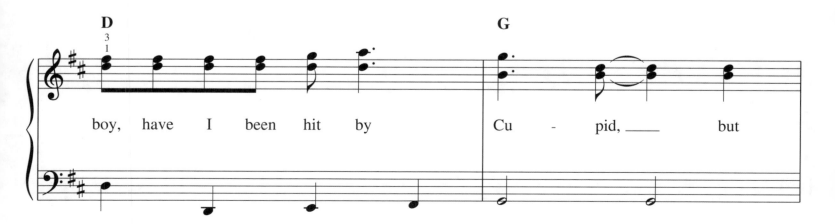

WHOSE BED HAVE YOUR BOOTS BEEN UNDER?

Words and Music by SHANIA TWAIN
and R.J. LANGE

Whose bed have your boots been un - der?

Whose bed have your boots been un - der?

And whose heart did you steal, I won - der?

Copyright © 1995 Songs Of PolyGram International, Inc., Loon Echo, Inc. and Out Of Pocket Productions Ltd.
All Rights on behalf of Out Of Pocket Productions Ltd. Controlled by Zomba Enterprises Inc. for the U.S. and Canada
International Copyright Secured   All Rights Reserved

61

62

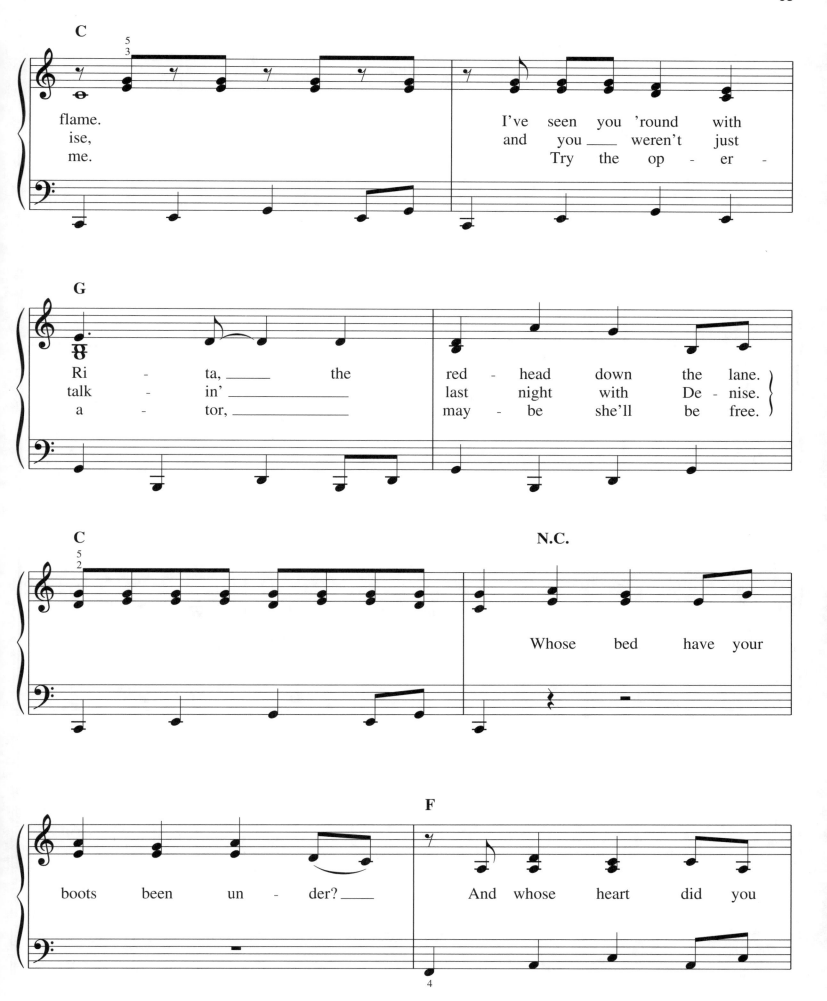

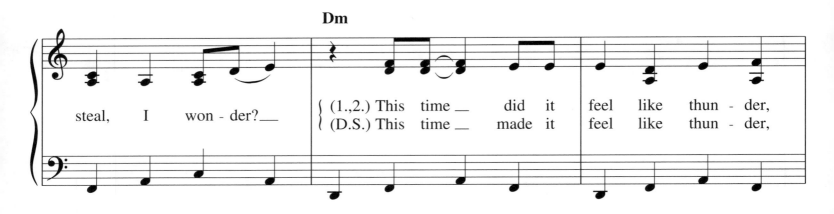

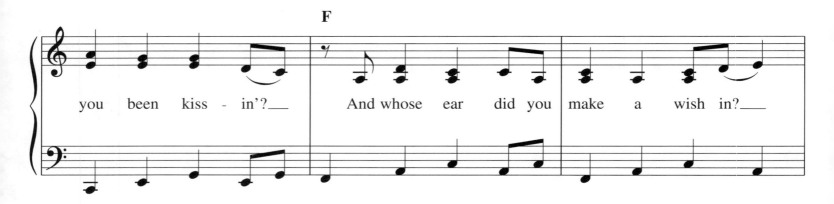

THE WOMAN IN ME
(Needs the Man in You)

Words and Music by SHANIA TWAIN
and R.J. LANGE

Copyright © 1995 Songs Of PolyGram International, Inc., Loon Echo, Inc. and Out Of Pocket Productions Ltd.
All Rights on behalf of Out Of Pocket Productions Ltd. Controlled by Zomba Enterprises Inc. for the U.S. and Canada
International Copyright Secured   All Rights Reserved

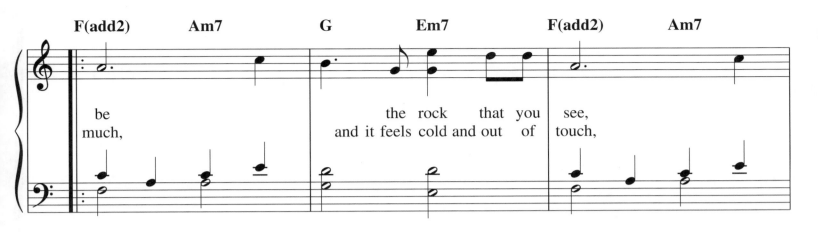

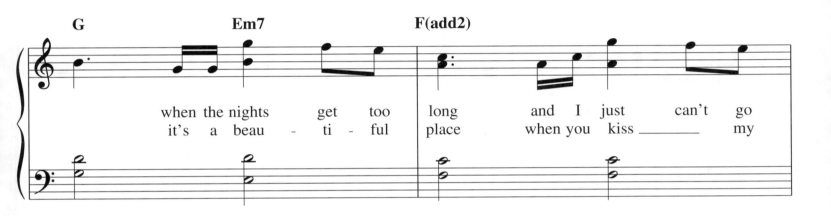

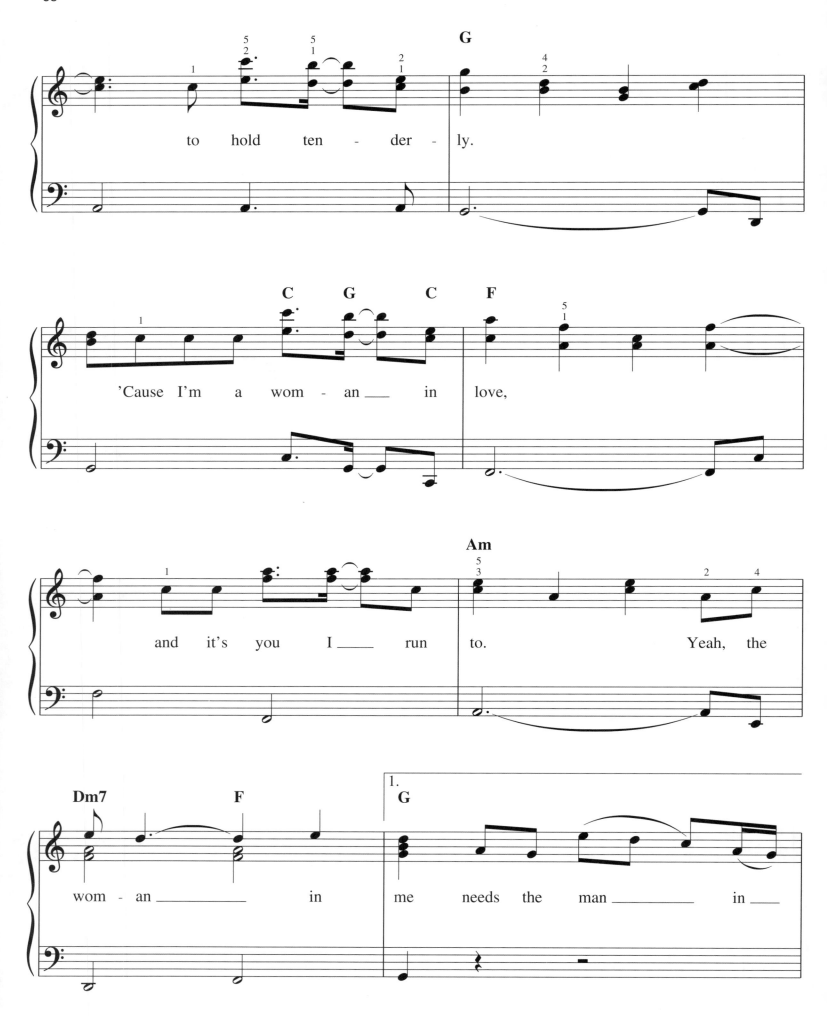

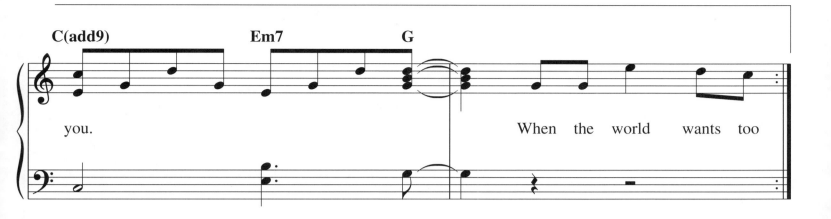

you.   When   the   world   wants   too

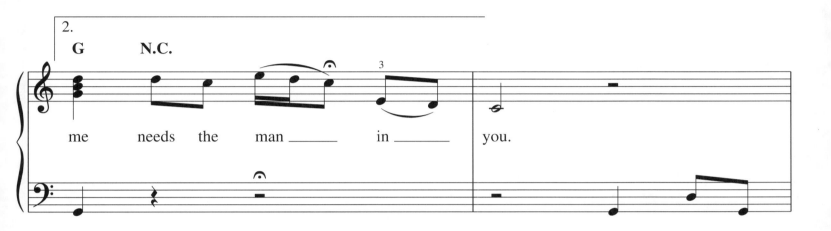

2.
me   needs   the   man _____ in _____   you.

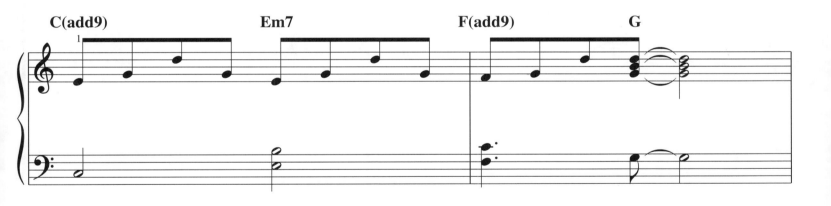

YOU'RE STILL THE ONE

Words and Music by SHANIA TWAIN
and R.J. LANGE

Copyright © 1997 Songs Of PolyGram International, Inc., Loon Echo, Inc. and Out Of Pocket Productions Ltd.
All Rights on behalf of Out Of Pocket Productions Ltd. Controlled by Zomba Enterprises Inc. for the U.S. and Canada
International Copyright Secured   All Rights Reserved

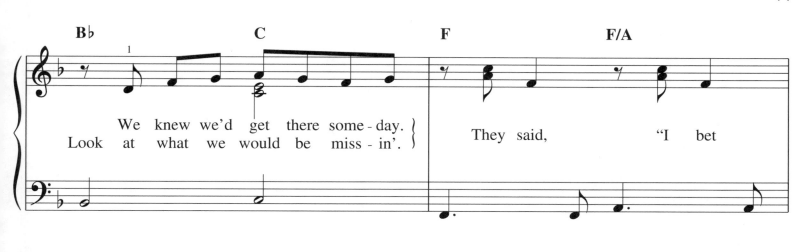

We knew we'd get there some-day.
Look at what we would be miss-in'.
They said, "I bet

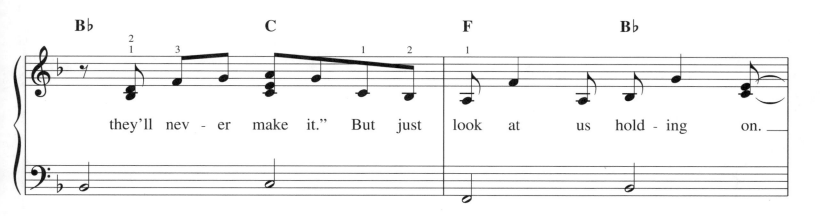

they'll nev - er make it." But just look at us hold - ing on.

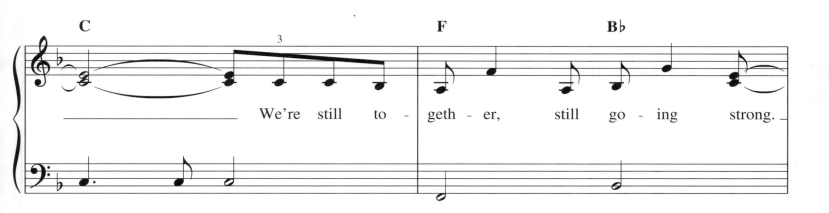

We're still to - geth - er, still go - ing strong.

(You're still the one.) You're still the one I run to,

72